Wars Waged Under the Microscope

The War Against COVID-19

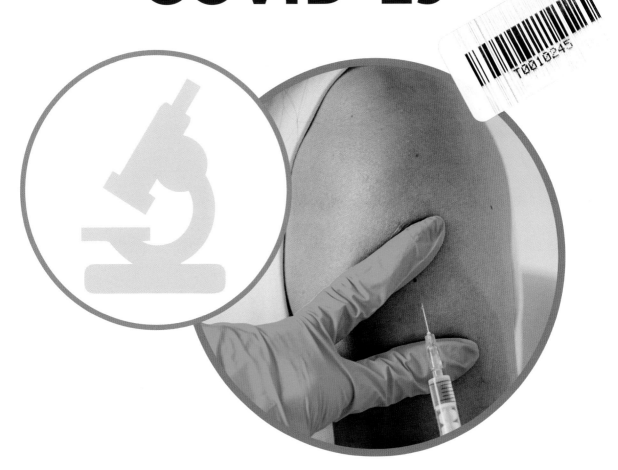

Cynthia O'Brien

CRABTREE
PUBLISHING COMPANY
WWW.CRABTREEBOOKS.COM

CRABTREE
PUBLISHING COMPANY
WWW.CRABTREEBOOKS.COM

Author: Cynthia O'Brien

Editors: Sarah Eason, Jennifer Sanderson, and Ellen Rodger

Editorial director: Kathy Middleton

Design: Simon Borrough

Cover design and additional artwork: Katherine Berti

Photo research: Rachel Blount

Proofreader: Wendy Scavuzzo

Production coordinator and Prepress technician: Ken Wright

Print coordinator: Katherine Berti

Consultant: David Hawksett

Produced for Crabtree Publishing by Calcium Creative Ltd

Library and Archives Canada Cataloguing in Publication

Title: The war against COVID-19 / Cynthia O'Brien.
Names: O'Brien, Cynthia (Cynthia J.), author.
Description: Series statement: Wars waged under the microscope | Includes bibliographical references and index.
Identifiers: Canadiana (print) 20210189096 |
   Canadiana (ebook) 2021018910X |
   ISBN 9781427151285 (hardcover) |
   ISBN 9781427151360 (softcover) |
   ISBN 9781427151445 (IITML) |
   ISBN 9781427151520 (EPUB)
Subjects: LCSH: COVID-19 (Disease)—Juvenile literature. |
   LCSH: COVID-19 (Disease)—Treatment—Juvenile literature. |
   LCSH: COVID-19 (Disease)—Prevention—Juvenile literature. |
   LCSH: Epidemics—Juvenile literature.
Classification: LCC RA644.C67 O27 2022 |
   DDC j614.5/92414—dc23

Library of Congress Cataloging-in-Publication Data

Names: O'Brien, Cynthia (Cynthia J.) author.
Title: The war against COVID-19 / Cynthia O'Brien.
Description: New York, NY : Crabtree Publishing Company, [2022] | Series: Wars waged under the microscope | Includes index.
Identifiers: LCCN 2021016669 (print) |
   LCCN 2021016670 (ebook) |
   ISBN 9781427151285 (hardcover) |
   ISBN 9781427151360 (paperback) |
   ISBN 9781427151445 (ebook) |
   ISBN 9781427151520 (epub)
Subjects: LCSH: COVID-19 (Disease)--Juvenile literature. |
   COVID-19 (Disease)--Treatment--Juvenile literature. |
   COVID-19 (Disease)--Prevention--Juvenile literature. |
   Epidemics--Juvenile literature.
Classification: LCC RA644.C67 O27 2022 (print) |
   LCC RA644.C67 (ebook) | DDC 614.5/92414--dc23
LC record available at https://lccn.loc.gov/2021016669
LC ebook record available at https://lccn.loc.gov/2021016670

Crabtree Publishing Company
www.crabtreebooks.com 1-800-387-7650

Printed in the U.S.A./062021/CG20210401

Published in Canada
Crabtree Publishing
616 Welland Ave.
St. Catharines, Ontario
L2M 5V6

Published in the United States
Crabtree Publishing
347 Fifth Ave.
Suite 1402-145
New York, NY 10016

Contents

The Enemy

In late 2019, a deadly disease emerged in China. By March 2020, the world was in the grips of a **pandemic**. The disease is called COVID-19 and it is caused by a **virus** that scientists had never seen before. The virus that causes COVID-19 is a novel, or new, type of coronavirus.

What Is a Coronavirus?

Coronaviruses are a large family of viruses that can affect birds, and **mammals**, including humans. Many coronaviruses cause mild illnesses, such as some common colds. Coronaviruses generally target the upper **respiratory system**, including the nose and throat. However, the new coronavirus, SARS-CoV-2, which causes COVID-19, can also attack the lungs. It can then go on to affect other **organs**.

The coronavirus that causes COVID-19 may have transferred to humans from pangolins. Pangolins are anteater-like mammals that are sold illegally for food and medicine in markets in China.

Coronaviruses spread quickly in large crowds where people are close together.

A Deadly Spread

Virologist Shi Zhengli and her team were the first to identify SARS-CoV-2. They tested fluid **samples** taken from patients in Wuhan, China, who had a mysterious case of **pneumonia**. They discovered that a new coronavirus caused the illness. It was very similar to one Shi had earlier found in bats. Shi believed that the virus had passed from a bat to another animal then to a human. No one is sure what animal the bat infected before the virus passed to people.

The new coronavirus spread quickly, infecting thousands of people in China, then around the world within months. Governments and scientists urgently looked for ways to prevent it, and they began developing treatments and **vaccines**. On March 11, 2020, the **World Health Organization (WHO)** declared a pandemic. By that time, there were 118,000 cases in 114 countries. By December 2020, there were more than 73 million cases and more than 1.6 million deaths worldwide.

"We have a choice. Can we come together to face a common and dangerous enemy?"

Tedros Adhanom Ghebreyesus, Director-General, WHO

The Battle Begins

The first cases of COVID-19 emerged in Wuhan, China. By December 1, several people had become very sick with pneumonia, but doctors did not know what triggered the infection in the first place. Then they discovered they were dealing with something new. This was the beginning of the war against COVID-19.

Looking at History

There are hundreds of different coronaviruses that scientists know about. However, only seven of these, including SARS-CoV-2, infect humans. Scientists looked back at other coronavirus **outbreaks** for clues about the new virus. They knew that coronaviruses usually started in animals, and that the coronaviruses that infect people usually infect animals first.

Different types of bats carry about 60 viruses that can infect humans. Bats live close together, making it easy for the virus to spread.

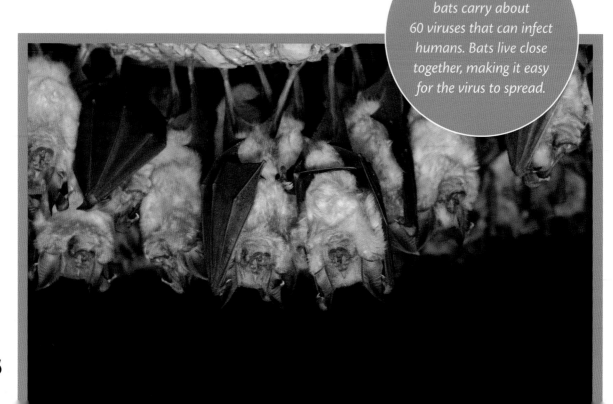

Other Coronaviruses

In 2003, a coronavirus caused the Severe Acute Respiratory Syndrome (SARS). It spread from China to other countries. People became sick with a high **fever** and other symptoms, or signs of illness. The virus likely started in bats and transferred to another animal before infecting humans. In 2012, another coronavirus caused the Middle East Respiratory Syndrome (MERS). The first cases of MERS were in Saudi Arabia, but the virus spread to more than 25 other countries. People caught the virus from camels and the camels likely got it from bats. MERS causes fever and coughing, and often turns into pneumonia.

Early Battles

Scientists first thought that, like other coronaviruses, SARS-CoV-2 mainly attacked the respiratory system. They saw that the virus was very contagious, or spread easily from person to person. It was able to infect the throat or lungs quickly. If the virus latched onto lung **cells**, it could do a lot of damage. Some people's **immune systems** could stop this, but in other cases, patients do not recover.

COVID-19 cases soared and hospitals ran out of room. Medical workers cared for patients in temporary field hospitals, like this one in New York.

An Invisible Threat

Coronavirus is a microorganism, also called a microbe. Microbes exist in plants, water, soil, and the human body. They cannot be seen without a microscope, yet they are all around. A microscope is a device that magnifies things, or makes them bigger.

Pathogens on the Attack

Types of **bacteria**, viruses, **fungi**, and **protozoa** are all pathogens. Pathogens are microbes that can cause many different diseases. For example, bacteria can cause throat infections. Fungi can trigger skin infections, while a protozoan, carried by some mosquitoes, is responsible for malaria.

Viruses are the tiniest microbes. There are many kinds of viruses, most of them causing diseases, from chickenpox and colds to influenza and COVID-19. Viruses cannot exist or spread on their own. They need to invade cells in living things to thrive. Then they use the cells to replicate, or make copies of, themselves. These copies spread to other cells. As the virus attacks, it kills, damages, or changes the cells, causing people to become sick.

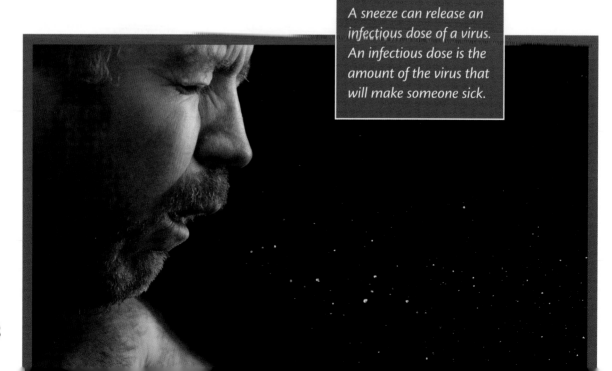

A sneeze can release an infectious dose of a virus. An infectious dose is the amount of the virus that will make someone sick.

Soap and water make most viruses fall apart and become inactive. This is why it is important for people to wash their hands often.

How People Catch Viruses

Viruses enter the human body in a variety of ways. They can spread from person to person through tiny droplets in the air or through contaminated, or impure, water or food. Some viruses live on surfaces for a period of time. The coronavirus that causes COVID-19 usually transfers through droplets in the air. Droplets may come from an infected person coughing, talking, or sneezing, and others may breathe in the droplets. The virus may land on surfaces and stay active for a time. People may pick up the virus and transfer it to their noses or mouths when they touch their faces.

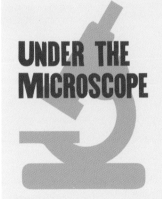

UNDER THE MICROSCOPE

Viruses are so tiny that scientists could not identify them until they had powerful microscopes. In the 1890s, scientists identified the tobacco mosaic virus that infected the tobacco plant. Later research began detecting viruses that infected humans. Today, virologists know about more than 200 of these viruses, but they discover new viruses all the time.

Under Attack

COVID-19 is unpredictable. While most people have mild symptoms, some people end up in the hospital and the disease can be deadly. Many other people never get sick at all, even though they have the virus.

Early Signs

Often, the first signs of COVID-19 are a dry cough and fever. People may have difficulty breathing and feel very tired. Some people report losing their sense of taste and smell. COVID-19 symptoms can appear between 2 and 14 days from the time someone comes into contact with the virus. This is called the incubation period. However, as many as one in five infected people never have any COVID-19 symptoms.

Scientists are still studying when and for how long people are infectious. People with milder symptoms may infect others for about 10 days after they first feel sick. Others who are very sick with COVID-19 may be infectious for 20 days. This is why people who have COVID-19 go into **quarantine**. This helps stop the virus from spreading.

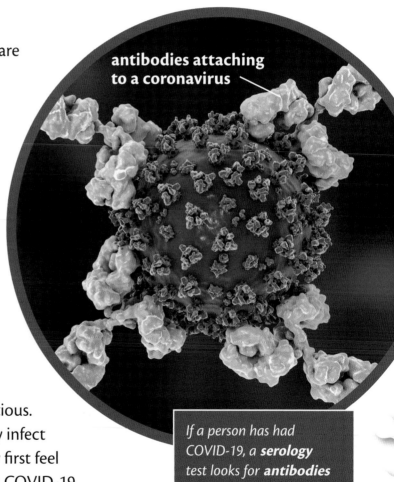

antibodies attaching to a coronavirus

*If a person has had COVID-19, a **serology** test looks for **antibodies** in a blood sample. The body would have created antibodies to fight the SARS-CoV-2 virus infection.*

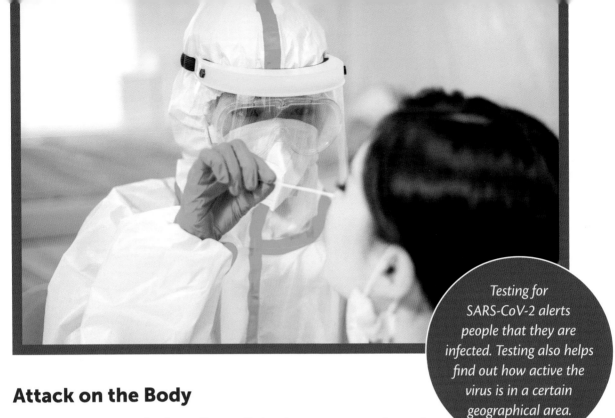

Attack on the Body

SARS-CoV-2 starts by invading cells in the nose, mouth, and throat. This causes symptoms such as fever. But the virus can go farther, invading cells in the lungs, liver, heart, and brain. Sometimes, the body's immune system overreacts and can make things worse. COVID-19 can also affect blood cells, leading to **strokes** and heart attacks. Most people recover well from COVID-19, but others have health issues a long time afterward.

UNDER THE MICROSCOPE

The first accurate tests for COVID-19 used a **mucus** sample taken with a **swab** inserted high in the nose. Other tests were developed to take samples from the throat or mouth. A lab tests the sample for evidence of the virus. Rapid tests can check saliva and give results in minutes.

War on COVID-19

At the end of January 2020, there were three known cases of COVID-19 in Italy. By March 11, when the WHO declared a pandemic, Italy had more than 10,000 cases. The virus spread quickly, especially among Italy's elderly population.

COVID-19 Hotspots

In the United States, the state of New York had its first known COVID-19 case on March 1, 2020. By April 2, the state had more than 92,000 cases and more than 2,500 deaths. The numbers were higher than the recorded cases in China. Many of the cases were in New York City. The number of hospital patients soared, and there was not enough room in the hospitals. By April, COVID-19 was widespread throughout the United States and Canada.

In spring 2020, tents like these in Italy became temporary emergency rooms. Retired doctors, nurses, and medics helped cover the shortage of medical workers.

CASE STUDY: THE SOUTH KOREAN STRATEGY

South Korea recorded its first COVID-19 case on January 20, 2020. By the end of February, there were thousands of cases. The country responded to the crisis with thorough testing. Health care workers tested people at drive-through sites and in hundreds of clinics. By the middle of April, more than 530,000 people had been tested for the virus. The tests were processed quickly, people were sent into quarantine, and the people they had been in contact with were traced. Contact tracing means finding out the names and locations of everyone who may have been near a person who tests positive for SARS-CoV-2. To do this, the South Koreans used modern technology, including smart phones and looking at credit card usage. The strategy was so successful that the system could locate about 1,000 possibly infected people in just an hour. However, the system did involve tapping into people's privacy through their phones and other data. Through contact tracing, South Korea was able to bring the virus under control and, unlike many other countries, it did not have to close its businesses.

When a new surge of cases broke out in August 2020, the government ordered more testing, and people were told to keep apart and wear masks. Almost 2,000 schools closed. Within a few weeks, the virus was under control again.

Tracing apps help track the spread of COVID-19. Using location services, the app records where people are. If someone tests positive and is in the same location, the app sends an alert to those in the area.

A Tiny Enemy

Microbiologists are scientists who study microbes such as viruses and bacteria. When the SARS-CoV-2 virus was discovered, scientists began to study ways to defeat this microscopic enemy.

How a Coronavirus Invades

Viruses are about 100 times smaller than a human cell. No virus can spread unless it invades a cell, so they need a way to get in. The coronavirus that causes COVID-19 uses parts called proteins to attach to proteins made by human cells. This allows the virus to "unlock" the cell and take over.

Once inside the cell, the virus releases ribonucleic acid (RNA). RNA carries information about the virus. The infected human cell takes this information to start making copies of the virus. Each infected cell can make and release millions of copies of the virus. The cell dies and these copies go on to infect other cells.

This microscope image shows the SARS-CoV-2 virus. Its proteins are between 10 and 20 times more likely to bind to cell proteins than the SARS virus. This means that it is better at multiplying and spreading than the SARS virus.

Virus Highways

Using a powerful **electron microscope**, researchers discovered another feature of SARS-CoV-2. The scientists used infected monkey cells for their experiments because these cells react in a similar way to human cells. The infected cells grew long branches, called filopodia, which poke out. Sometimes, healthy cells also send out filopodia, but this can be to help repair other cells. The SARS-CoV-2 virus uses filopodia for a different reason. The branches break into nearby cells and provide quick paths for the virus to spread into these cells. This also means that the virus can infect many different cells at once.

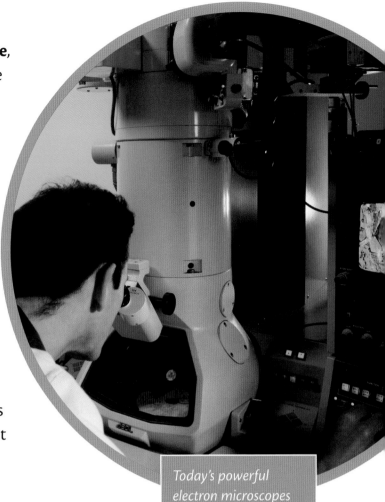

Today's powerful electron microscopes can magnify a sample 30,000 to 90,000 times.

UNDER THE MICROSCOPE

The word "corona" comes from the Latin word for crown. Coronaviruses get their name from their spiky surface, which looks a little like a crown. These viruses are so tiny that scientists can only see them using an electron microscope. The microscope produces colored pictures so they are easier to see.

Studying the Enemy

Microbiologists, epidemiologists, and infectious disease experts all study pathogens. Their studies and experiments lead to developing treatments and vaccines. They also help the world prepare to battle any new threats.

A Safe Place

To study pathogens like the SARS-CoV-2 virus, microbiologists work in high-containment biosafety level 3 labs. Containment means that the labs keep the virus from escaping. The biosafety level indicates the danger of the pathogen being studied. The highest biosafety level is 4. The labs keep the scientists safe while working with contagious, and possibly deadly, pathogens. Experiments are not done out in the open. When working with live or active pathogens, scientists do their work in biosafety cabinets. These are designed to **filter** the air going into and out of the cabinet. Viruses like SARS-CoV-2 release into the air, so the cabinet filters clean this air while the scientists are working.

By studying infected cells, virologists hope to understand how the virus multiplies so they can develop treatments to stop it.

CASE STUDY: A COVID-19 EXPERT

A virologist in Germany named Christian Drosten has been studying coronaviruses for many years. In 2003, Drosten helped design the first test for the coronavirus that causes SARS. After SARS, Drosten began studying the way the coronavirus evolves, or changes. Then, when MERS struck in 2012, everyone turned to Drosten and his lab.

In January 2020, the German researchers were already studying the SARS-CoV-2 virus in detail. Drosten and his colleagues created a test for the virus. From this development, countries around the world began making and using tests. With a reliable test, virologists went on to study how the virus transferred from person to person. They could also use the tests to understand how the virus affected patients.

Researchers tested nine patients every day from the first symptoms appearing and up to 28 days later. The scientists collected mucus, blood, and urine samples. Testing these samples showed that, once a person had breathed in the virus, it could start multiplying in the throat, before traveling to the lungs. The virus could then be easily transmitted into the air and infect another person. This is one of the reasons COVID-19 is so contagious, especially soon after people are infected.

Scientists do not enter the lab before putting on protective clothing. In addition, they wear respirators that blow pure air into the hoods of their suits as they work.

Armed with Medicine

Viruses are different from one another and do not all respond to the same medicines. Even small differences between them mean that a medicine or vaccination for one may not work for another. This is a great challenge in fighting them.

Antiviral Medicine

Antiviral drugs are used to help treat viruses. In most cases, antivirals are not a cure, but they can make people feel better. Some antivirals can help stop a virus from invading other cells. However, creating antivirals can be difficult because the antiviral should kill only the virus and not the cells.

There are no approved antiviral medications specifically for COVID-19. Instead, doctors have turned to antivirals used for other diseases. These seem to work best before the virus has had a chance to multiply too much. At the same time, scientists are looking for new treatments and ways to develop them. For example, researchers are studying human cells and what makes them vulnerable to a virus takeover.

The hope is to find treatments that work for COVID-19 that may work for any new coronavirus outbreaks in the future.

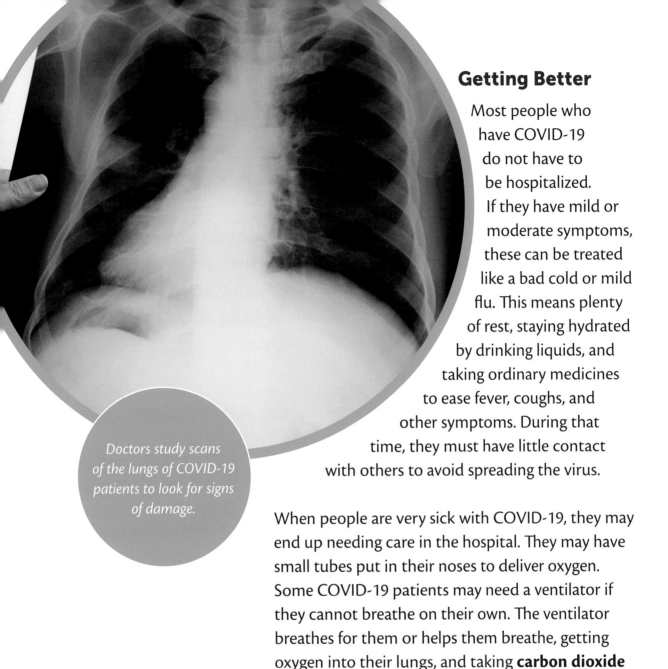

Doctors study scans of the lungs of COVID-19 patients to look for signs of damage.

Getting Better

Most people who have COVID-19 do not have to be hospitalized. If they have mild or moderate symptoms, these can be treated like a bad cold or mild flu. This means plenty of rest, staying hydrated by drinking liquids, and taking ordinary medicines to ease fever, coughs, and other symptoms. During that time, they must have little contact with others to avoid spreading the virus.

When people are very sick with COVID-19, they may end up needing care in the hospital. They may have small tubes put in their noses to deliver oxygen. Some COVID-19 patients may need a ventilator if they cannot breathe on their own. The ventilator breathes for them or helps them breathe, getting oxygen into their lungs, and taking **carbon dioxide** out of their bodies.

" *...the more you understand about the biology of the virus, the more powerful you are with respect to treatments.* "

Dr. Nevan Krogan, Molecular Biologist, University of California, Quantitative Biosciences Institute

Taking It to the Front Line

Testing and treating people with COVID-19 takes an army of healthcare and lab workers in every country. They are at the front line of the war against COVID-19, trying to stop the virus from spreading, and dealing with millions of sick patients.

Staying Safe

The first line of defense against COVID-19 is to stop the virus from entering the body in the first place. Doctors, nurses, and others who deal with infected people must wear personal protective equipment (PPE). These protective coverings are vital for safety.

Everyone else can do their part to slow the spread of the virus by wearing masks in public spaces, especially indoors. Cleaning surfaces, frequent handwashing, and social distancing are also important weapons in the fight against COVID-19. Social distancing means keeping a safe distance of at least 6 feet (2 m) when out in public. Keeping hands and surfaces clean and not touching the face help keep the virus from infecting the body and from spreading the disease to others.

Wearing a mask, especially indoors or if people are close together, helps protect others from the virus.

Stopping the Spread

During the 2020 pandemic, people stopped traveling from one country to another. Testing clinics opened everywhere, and hospitals geared up to take patients. Lockdown measures meant that people stayed home, except to buy food or other vital supplies. Restaurants, stores, and other businesses closed for weeks or months at a time. Only hospitals, grocery stores, and other necessary services stayed open. Many schools closed, too. In some places, children had lessons online. Where there was a high number of COVID-19 cases, only people who lived together could spend time with each other. This meant that children and adults could not see friends or other family members for weeks or months at a time.

When schools are closed, many students have to learn online at home instead.

UNDER THE MICROSCOPE

The "R" value of a virus relates to how it reproduces. The flu has an R number of about 1.3. The SARS-CoV-2 virus has a reproduction number of about 3 or higher. So, if 100 people are infected, they could infect 300 people, who could then infect 900 people, and so on.

Fighting Back

To fight deadly viruses, virologists develop vaccines. This can take many years because scientists must perform research as well as many tests to make sure the vaccine will work on people and be safe.

Developing a Vaccine

Most vaccines are created from a dead or very weak form of a pathogen. The vaccine tricks the immune system into reacting as it would to a real threat. The body responds by making antibodies to fight the invading **antigens**. Then, if the immune system meets these invaders again, it remembers them and creates antibodies right away. This response protects people from future infection. Vaccines may not work for everyone. Even so, if most people are given a vaccine, it helps keep the pathogen from spreading through the population.

COVID-19 vaccines do not use a form of the virus. Instead, mRNA vaccines instruct the body's cells to make a harmless spike protein. The immune system starts creating antibodies, just as it would respond to a COVID-19 spike protein.

CASE STUDY: WORKING TOGETHER

By April 2020, almost 80 different companies in 19 countries were working on COVID-19 vaccines. By the fall, scientists were working on more than 150 potential vaccines.

After a vaccine is developed and tested in a lab, there are usually three stages of **clinical trials**. In the first phase, small groups of volunteers receive the vaccine. The scientists check to see if the volunteers' immune systems have created antibodies to respond to the vaccine. In the second phase, the trials involve people who may be more vulnerable to the disease and need the vaccine the most. In the third phase, thousands of people receive the vaccine and are monitored closely.

*The first tests of any vaccine are done on **cell cultures**, then on animals, such as mice. They are monitored for any **side effects.***

Each country has its own government department to handle this process of trials. In the United States, the Food and Drug Administration (FDA) approves vaccines. The FDA will not approve a vaccine unless it is proven to be at least 50 percent effective, meaning that it works for at least half the people in the trial. Even after a vaccine is approved, scientists continue to monitor it. In December 2020, the FDA approved the first COVID-19 vaccine.

New Weapons

Dealing with COVID-19 has changed the world in many ways. During the first few months of the 2020 pandemic, learning online and working from home became common. Online parties, concerts, and meetings took the place of meeting in person. For people around the world, these changes became part of a new way of living.

Living with COVID-19

There is no cure for COVID-19. However, new treatments and vaccines will help keep the disease under control. Many treatments are in development or in clinical trials. Some are antivirals that work to stop the virus from invading or stop it from multiplying. Others try to trick the virus. For example, scientists are creating artificial proteins that may bind to the virus and keep it from infecting cells. The body's immune system is very powerful, so many people do not need extra treatments to fight COVID-19. The antibodies they produce may help others, though, so scientists are also looking at ways to use them in their treatment of very sick people.

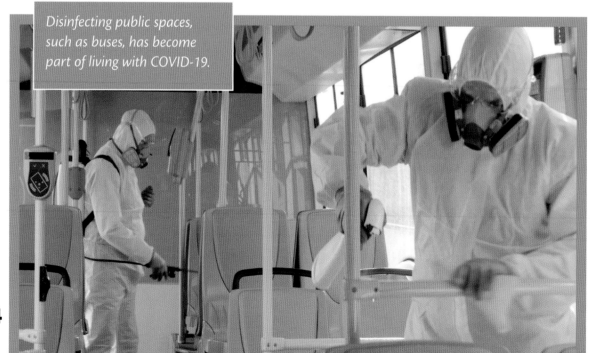

Disinfecting public spaces, such as buses, has become part of living with COVID-19.

New Technology

Scientists are developing different tools to find out where the SARS-CoV-2 virus may be lurking. New technology may be able to detect the SARS-CoV-2 virus in the air and work as a warning system for indoor spaces. Other machines may be used to disinfect the air, wiping out any **airborne** coronaviruses.

Other technology may help make sure that treatments are safe. One way to do that is to create a **clone** of the SARS-CoV-2 virus. This is called a replicon. It would not be infectious, so it would be safe to handle. There would be no need for scientists to use a specialized lab, making it easier and faster for scientists to work. If scientists could create a SARS-CoV-2 replicon, they could test new medicines as they become available.

Researchers are investigating the use of sniffer dogs to detect COVID-19. In trials, the dogs detected the virus before people had symptoms.

Future Warfare

The fight against COVID-19 is still new. Scientists will be looking for better treatments and closely studying the virus to spot any changes. They will also be on the lookout for any new coronaviruses or other threats, to be prepared for any future outbreaks.

Long-Term Effects

Scientists are studying the ongoing health of COVID-19 patients. This will help them understand how the virus affects the body after patients have recovered and no longer carry the virus. Researchers also look at people's ages and overall health. The virus infects people of all ages, even if they do not have other health conditions. Important research will study how COVID-19 affects children's future health.

Some patients still have problems months after they first become sick. They may suffer extreme tiredness or still have problems breathing. COVID-19 can affect much more of the body than expected, including the heart and brain. One idea is that the coronavirus may trigger a cytokine storm in the immune system. This means that the immune system overreacts when it is trying to protect the body. So, instead of helping the body, the immune system actually hurts it.

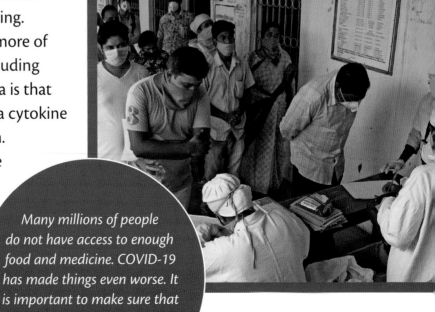

Many millions of people do not have access to enough food and medicine. COVID-19 has made things even worse. It is important to make sure that everyone gets the help they need to survive.

Keeping Everyone Safe

Even with a vaccine, it will be difficult and expensive to keep everyone safe. The Coalition for Epidemic Preparedness Innovations (CEPI) launched in 2017. The organization supports the development of vaccines and became involved when COVID-19 became a threat. In addition, many countries signed up for the COVID-19 Vaccines Global Access (COVAX). By agreeing to the plan, richer countries commit to paying for vaccine doses for their own country and for poorer countries that cannot afford to pay. For the plan to work, it needs countries to contribute billions of dollars.

Another worldwide program is Access to COVID-19 Tools (ACT). The program brought together organizations such as the WHO, World Bank, and the Bill & Melinda Gates Foundation. ACT began at the end of April 2020 as a way to support developing tests, treatments, and vaccines.

The COVID-19 pandemic created a worldwide army of scientists who are working together as never before.

"
. . . .

"Access to a life-saving vaccine shouldn't depend on where you live or how much money you have. The development and approval of a safe and effective vaccine is crucial, but equally important is making sure the vaccines are available and affordable to everyone. COVID-19 anywhere is COVID-19 everywhere."

Robert Silverman, Oxfam America

. . . .

Timeline

Since the first identification of SARS-CoV-2, the world has come together to fight this tiny enemy. From widespread testing to developing vaccines, science has been at the forefront of this war.

December 2019	China warns the WHO of mysterious cases of pneumonia.
January 2, 2020	China reports 44 cases of patients with pneumonia caused by the new virus.
January 9, 2020	The WHO announces that the new virus has been identified as SARS-CoV-2.
January 11, 2020	First known death from SARS-CoV-2 in Wuhan, China, is reported.
January 13, 2020	Thailand has the first SARS-CoV-2 case outside of China.
January 16, 2020	A lab in Germany develops the first diagnostic test for the virus.
January 21, 2020	The first confirmed case of COVID-19 in the United States is reported.
January 30, 2020	The WHO declares a Public Health Emergency of International Concern (PHEIC) with more than 9,000 cases worldwide.

February 11, 2020	Scientists gather in Geneva, Switzerland, to share knowledge and agree on a way to work together to fight SARS-CoV-2. The disease it causes is named COVID-19.
February 26, 2020	Remdesivir, an antiviral drug developed for Ebola, is trialled in the United States as a treatment for COVID-19.
February 29, 2020	The United States expands testing for COVID-19.
March 11, 2020	The WHO declares a pandemic as cases reach more than 100,000 worldwide.
March 19, 2020	California becomes the first state in the USA to issue a stay-at-home order.
May 22, 2020	*The Lancet* medical journal reports that the first COVID-19 vaccine to be tested on humans is promising and found to produce an immune response in 14 days.
August 2020	China and Russia approve the early use of vaccines during Phase 3 trials.
December 2020	A 90-year-old woman in the United Kingdom (UK) is the first member of the public to have a COVID-19 vaccine shot.

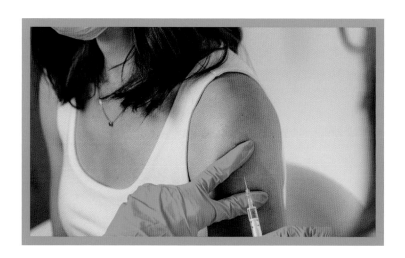

Glossary

airborne Carried through the air

antibodies Substances produced by the body that fight off invading bacteria and viruses

antigens Invaders in the body, such as viruses

bacteria Single-celled organisms that can cause disease

carbon dioxide A gas that is created through the process of breathing

cell cultures Cells removed from animal or plant tissue and grown in a laboratory

cells The smallest units of a living thing that can survive on their own, carrying out a range of life processes

clinical trials Research performed on people to discover more about disease treatment

clone An exact copy

electron microscope A high-powered microscope that uses beams of electrons instead of rays of light

epidemiologists Scientists that study the cause, spread, and control of disease

fever A high body temperature

filter To take pieces out of something, for example, to remove a virus from the air

fungi Living things that grow and feed on other living things

immune system The organs and other parts of the body that work together to protect it against sickness

mammals Animals with warm blood that feed their young with milk from their bodies

microorganism A small living thing that can only be seen with a microscope

mucus A slimy substance found in the body

organs Parts of the body, such as the heart and lungs, that have specific functions

outbreaks Infections of more than one person in a geographical region

pandemic Situation in which a disease spreads and affects people across the world

pneumonia A disease that affects the lungs and makes it difficult to breathe

protozoa Single-celled organisms that can live freely or as parasites

quarantine A period of time when a person with a disease is kept away from others to prevent the disease from spreading

respiratory system The set of organs that allows a person to breathe and exchange oxygen and carbon dioxide throughout the body

samples Small amounts of something, such as blood, for testing

serology The study or examination of blood samples

side effects Unpleasant effects that taking a certain drug has on a person, such as making them feel dizzy

strokes Dangerous conditions in which the blood supply to the brain is cut off

swab An absorbent pad that can be used by doctors to take samples

vaccines Substances that help protect against certain diseases

virologist A scientist who studies viruses

virus A microscopic organism that can cause sickness

World Health Organization (WHO) An organization that helps governments improve their health services

Learning More

Find out more about COVID-19 and how the war against this deadly disease is being won.

Books

Bradford Edwards, Sue. *Coronavirus: The COVID-19 Pandemic* (Special Reports). BDO Publishing, 2020.

DiLorenzo Williams, Heather. *A Lasting Impact* (COVID-19). Lerner Publications, 2020.

Farndon, John. *Tiny Killers : When Bacteria and Viruses Attack* (The Sickening History of Medicine). Hungry Tomato, 2017.

Hustad, Douglas. *Understanding COVID-19* (Core Library Guide to COVID-19). North Star Editions, 2020.

Websites

Read an online book that explains the coronavirus and how everyone can help stop the spread of COVID-19:
https://nosycrowcoronavirus.s3-eu-west-1.amazonaws.com/Coronavirus_ABookForChildren.pdf

Find out how vaccines are made by watching the video and reading at:
www.cbc.ca/kidsnews/post/watch-how-are-vaccines-made

Learn all the basics about the coronavirus that causes COVID-19 at:
www.natgeokids.com/au/discover/science/general-science/what-is-coronavirus

Check out an animated video the explains COVID-19 at:
www.youtube.com/watch?v=D9tTi-CDjDU

Index

ABOUT THE AUTHOR

Cynthia O'Brien has written many books for children, including books about science and how the human body works. Researching this book, she learned a lot about COVID-19 and the amazing work that microbiologists and others are doing in the fight against it.